Resurgence and Growth

of

Al-Qaeda terrorists

By

Paul Williamson

TABLE OF CONTENTS

Introduction

Osama bin Laden established the terrorist Sunni Islamist group Al Qaeda in the late 1980s. The US-led war on terror significantly weakened the group in the years that followed after it gained popularity following the September 11 attacks in the US in 2001. *Al Qaeda, however, is still active and has recently had a revival, particularly in the Indian subcontinent, Africa, and the Middle East.*

The protracted crisis in Syria and the development of the Islamic State of Iraq and Syria are two elements that have contributed to Al Qaeda's rebirth (ISIS). Al Qaeda has benefited from the unrest and instability in the area to increase its influence and attract new followers. An additional aspect is *a rising discontentment among Muslim youth in several nations with the political and economic circumstances they face. Some young people, looking for a sense of purpose and connection, have been motivated by this disenchantment to join extremist organizations like Al Qaeda.*

To spread its propaganda and find new members, *Al Qaeda has also been successful in utilizing contemporary technologies.*

For the gang to connect with its supporters and plan attacks, *social media sites and encrypted messaging applications have made this simpler.* **The senior U.S. counterterrorism** officer warns that **jihadi groups** like **al-Qaeda and Islamic State cannot be disregarded** as incidents like the **Buffalo, New York**, mass shooting in **May 2022 that left 10 Black shoppers dead** continue to make headlines and command the attention of authorities. "**ISIS** is a pretty nimble organization that is still steered from this core in **Iraq and Syria**, and they continue to be interested in not just maintaining their territorial integrity, but also in gaining publicity, growing their brand, and carrying out strikes against the West. One of the most dreaded jihadist terrorist groups in the world may not be on the verge of extinction, but rather, thanks to an unlikely friend, it may be set for a potential comeback.

The terror organization has built a new base of operations almost 20 years after the ***United States first targeted al-Qaeda in Afghanistan for orchestrating the September 11, 2001 attacks on New York's World Trade Center and the Pentagon.*** For months, American counterterrorism officials have been focusing less on domestic terrorist groups and more on those who are looking outside for ideologies to support their use of violence. The government's most recent terrorism advice states that individuals or small groups motivated by a variety of ideologies and grudges represent a "persistent and devastating threat to the homeland" and are the most likely attackers. Al Qaeda's revival is generally a worrying development for world security.

To oppose the group's ideology and activities and stop new assaults, governments and international organizations will need to keep cooperating.

Chapter 1

Al Qaeda's History and Origin

The Soviet-Afghan War in the 1980s is where **Al Qaeda first emerged.** When the **Soviet Union was still occupying Afghanistan**, (**Osama bin Laden**) was a successful Saudi businessman **who joined the mujahideen, a group of Muslim guerrilla fighters.** In addition to **creating a network of Arab fighters**

who traveled to Afghanistan to take part in the conflict.

Bin Laden utilized his money to fund the mujahideen.

Bin Laden and his supporters returned to Saudi Arabia in 1989 following the Soviet Union's withdrawal from Afghanistan. *They quickly lost hope in the Saudi administration, which they perceived as corrupt and too allied with the West.* **Bin Laden was driven out of Saudi Arabia and exiled to Sudan in 1991**. Bin Laden maintained his network of supporters, which he referred to as Al Qaeda, while he was in Sudan. The group considered the United States and its allies as Islam's enemies, and their mission was to fight jihad, or holy war, against them. Moreover, Bin Laden forged close relations with the Taliban, an extremist Islamist organization that had seized power in Afghanistan in 1996. Al Qaeda bombed the US embassies in Kenya and Tanzania simultaneously in 1998, killing 224 people and wounding thousands more. *This was the first of a string of assaults carried out by the group before the 9/11 attacks. Bin Laden and many of his top lieutenants fled Afghanistan after the US assault in 2001. The gang did execute assaults nonetheless, notably the 2004 and 2005 bombings in Madrid and London. In 2011, US forces ultimately tracked down and assassinated Bin Laden in Pakistan.*

Al Qaeda has suffered since the killing of bin Laden, but it still poses a threat.

Although the organization has split into various sections, its philosophy still serves as an inspiration for militants all over the world.

The Afghan-Soviet War and bin Laden's ascent.

The Soviet Union and the Afghan Mujahideen, who were backed by the United States, Pakistan, and other nations, fought a protracted war in Afghanistan from 1979 until 1989. Osama bin Laden and Al-Qaeda became more powerful as a result of the conflict, which had a profound effect on the area and the entire world. **The Soviet Union**

invaded Afghanistan during the conflict to back the communist regime that had seized control in a coup in 1978. ***With assistance from the United States and other nations***, the Mujahideen, a coalition of diverse Afghan resistance groups, battled against the Soviet army. The fight became known as "Soviet Vietnam" because of its similarities to the **Vietnam War**, including ***guerilla warfare, large-scale bombs, and political unrest***. A wealthy Saudi Arabian who supported the ***Mujahideen*** cause, ***Bin Laden*** went to Afghanistan to take part in the conflict with the Soviet Union.

He established the Maktab al-Khadamat (MAK), an organization whose mission was to support the Mujahideen militarily and financially. Bin Laden's reputation among the Mujahideen and their followers developed as a result of his bravery and leadership. *In 1989*, when the **Soviet Union left Afghanistan**, bin **Laden** went back to **Saudi Arabia** and started **working with the MAK**. However, he **lost faith** in the **Saudi leadership** and **started calling** for a

worldwide war against the West, including the United States.

He established Al-Qaeda in 1988, which rose to prominence for its terrorist assaults on Western targets, such as the **1998 bombings of the American embassies in Africa and the 2001 attacks on the Pentagon and World Trade Center.**

The United States and its allies had the chance to back the Mujahideen and thwart Soviet expansionism during the Afghan-Soviet War. It also had unexpected repercussions, such as the ***rise of Islamic extremism*** and the *establishment of Al-Qaeda* as a major international terrorist group.

The impacts of the war are still being felt today in the area and around the world.

The jihadist movement's global beginnings

The late 20th and early 21st centuries served as the movement's formative years. It is a complicated and comprehensive movement that incorporates several social, political, and religious elements. *Abdullah Azzam*, a Palestinian intellectual and ideologue who assisted in the establishment of the Afghan Arab network in the 1980s, was one of the most important and early figures in the global jihadist movement. *Azzam's lectures and writings encouraged many of these volunteers to take on a radical Islamist ideology.* This network gathered thousands of Arab volunteers to fight against the Soviet occupation of Afghanistan. ***Osama bin Laden, a powerful Saudi Arabian who fought alongside the Afghan mujahideen*** *in the 1980s* and later founded ***Al-Qaeda***, was a significant player in the growth of the global jihadist movement.

The goal of Bin Laden's global jihad movement was to oust Western hegemony and influence from the Muslim world. Several incidents in the **1990s** and **early 2000s**, such as *the Gulf War*, *The Israeli-Palestinian conflict*, and the **US-led invasion** of **Afghanistan in 2001**, further fueled the global jihadist movement. These incidents helped to shape the anti-Western and anti-modernist worldview of the movement and served as a breeding ground for jihadist ideology and recruitment. ***Al-Qaeda, the Islamic State of Iraq and Syria (ISIS)***, and various regional affiliates and offshoots are just a few of the groups and factions that make up today's global jihadist movement. The establishment of a global Islamic caliphate and the overthrow of Western influence and hegemony in the Muslim world remain the movement's ultimate goals, despite the movement's ongoing evolution and adaptation to shifting political and social conditions.

Chapter 2

Al Qaeda's Ideology

Al Qaeda's doctrine is founded on an extreme interpretation of Islam that calls for a world jihad, or holy war, against those it sees as Islam's adversaries, such as the United States and its allies. The ideology of Al Qaeda is based on the idea that the Muslim world is being attacked by Western nations, especially the United States, which wants to rule and dominate the area for its own economic and political purposes. Al Qaeda aspires to create a caliphate or Islamic state, that would unite all Muslims under its rule and sees itself as the defender of Islam against these aggressors. The idea of takfir the practice of labeling other Muslims as disbelievers or apostates is essential to Al Qaeda's doctrine. *Al Qaeda thinks that a lot of Muslim rulers and governments are dishonest, have deviated from the genuine precepts of Islam, and are hence not authentic Muslims.*

This justifies Al Qaeda's use of violence against non-Muslims seen as the enemy of Islam as well as other Muslims.

In addition, Al Qaeda subscribes to the Salafi-jihadist school of thought, which combines a strict application of Islamic law with the use of violent jihad to further its objectives. This ideology contends that to defend Islam and remove impediments to the development of an Islamic state, violent tactics must be employed. Al Qaeda wants to use terrorism to cause as much harm and casualties to its adversaries as possible in addition to achieving its religious and political objectives. These attacks aim to terrorize the populace, create instability, and cast doubt on the legitimacy of the institutions and governments that Al Qaeda considers to be its foes. Generally, the world community has denounced Al Qaeda's tactics as being violent and indiscriminate, and its ideology is founded on a combination of *religious fanaticism, anti-Western animosity, and militant jihadism.*

The Idea of Jihad and what it means to Al Qaeda

Jihad, which refers to the battle or endeavors to uphold righteousness in the world, is a key idea in Islam. Although the phrase is frequently used in armed conflict, its definition includes a variety of activities, including moral, intellectual, and spiritual ones.

The idea of jihad has been essential to Al Qaeda's ideology and its vision of a worldwide war against what it sees as the West and its supporters in the Middle East as enemies of Islam.

Al Qaeda sees jihad as a way to protect the Muslim ummah (community) from what it sees as non-Muslim oppression and violence. Al Qaeda's conception of jihad places a strong emphasis on armed conflict, and the organization has launched countless attacks in the name of jihad against both *civilian and military targets throughout the world. To establish a caliphate and purge Islam of what it perceives as Western influence and corruption, the* group sees itself as the forerunner of the global jihadist movement.

For Al Qaeda, the importance of jihad rests in its capacity to enthuse and mobilize its adherents as well as to justify its murderous deeds. *For the group's adherents, who consider themselves soldiers engaged in a just war, the word "jihad" acts as a rallying cry.*

Al Qaeda also aims to depict itself as a legitimate resistance movement against *foreign aggression and occupation by defining its operations as defensive jihad.*

Yet, *Muslim scholars and communities all around the world have strongly denounced using violence in the name of jihad.* **Many contend that Al Qaeda's actions go against the precepts of Islamic law**, which forbid violence against innocent people and attacks on civilian targets. *As a result, the group's strategies have drawn harsh criticism, even from some radical Islamist organizations*, leading to widespread condemnation of its doctrine and behavior.

Chapter 3

The World Network of Al Qaeda

The worldwide network of Al Qaeda consists of associated organizations, cells, and people who support its philosophy and objectives. These organizations, which are also known as **"Al Qaeda franchises," are active throughout the Middle East, Africa, South Asia, and Southeast Asia.**

The following are some of the most notable Al Qaeda associates:

*Al Qaeda in the Arabian Peninsula (AQAP): This organization has carried out high-profile **attacks in Yemen and Saudi Arabia**, including the attempted **bombing of an American airliner in 2009.***

*Al Qaeda in the Islamic Maghreb (AQIM): This North African organization has carried out multiple assaults in **Mali, Algeria**, and other **nations.***

*Al Qaeda in Syria (AQIS): This organization is active **in Syria** and is* *connected to the **Al Nusra Front**, which was once known as Al Qaeda's branch in Syria before **changing its name to Jabhat Fateh al-Sham in 2016.***

*Al Qaeda in the Indian Subcontinent (**AQIS**) was established in 2014 and conducts operations **in Bangladesh, Pakistan, and India.***

AQISIL, *also known as Al Qaeda in the Islamic State of Iraq and the Levant: This organization was established **in 2013 and works in Syria and Iraq.***

Al Qaeda has inspired and funded a large number of individuals and small groups who carry out attacks in its name in addition to these affiliates. Al Qaeda continues to pose a danger to international security due to its fragmented network, which makes it challenging to trace and target.

The organizational structure of Al Qaeda

Al Qaeda is a dispersed Islamist extremist organization, making it challenging to pinpoint its organizational structure.

Its organizational structure has changed over time in reaction to outside factors including government counterterrorism initiatives and the demise or capture of important leaders.

The Shura Council, a body of senior executives who make strategic decisions and offer direction to regional affiliates, sits at the apex of Al Qaeda's organizational structure. There are thought to be twelve people on the council, including **Ayman al-Zawahiri**, who is currently in charge of Al Qaeda. *Regional affiliates such as Al Qaeda in the Arabian Peninsula (AQAP), Al Qaeda in the Islamic Maghreb (AQIM), and Al Qaeda* in the Indian Subcontinent are included below the *Shura Council (AQIS)*. Although they primarily function autonomously, these affiliates have the same objective of undermining Western interests and advancing a radical Islamic agenda.

Each regional branch is further divided into cells or smaller units that do particular tasks, such as organizing and carrying out terrorist activities.

To reduce the possibility of being discovered and apprehended by law enforcement and intelligence organizations, these cells are frequently compartmentalized.

The organizational structure of Al Qaeda also consists of a network of financiers and intermediaries who support the group's operations with money and supplies.

This network frequently lacks centralized control and uses unofficial channels like *hawala* to conduct business (*traditional Islamic banking systems*).

Al Qaeda's organizational structure is made to be adaptable and versatile, enabling it to function in many areas and react to shifting conditions. Governments also have a tough time monitoring and halting the group's actions because of its decentralized character.

The function of Al Qaeda's regional affiliates and allies

Al-Qaida is a transnational terrorist group that seeks to establish a strict

Islamic state. **Operating in several regions of the world, such as the Middle East, South Asia, North Africa, and the Horn of Africa**, the organization has regional affiliates and allies.

Al-regional Qaeda's affiliates are organizations that have sworn allegiance to Ayman al-Zawahiri and carry out his orders.

These organizations are active in various regions of the globe and have differing degrees of ties to al-central Qaida's leadership.

Many of Qaeda's regional affiliates include.

Al-Qaeda in the Arabian Peninsula (AQAP): AQAP is one of almost all of Qaida's active and dangerous affiliates and is based in Yemen. AQAP has been implicated in several well-known assaults, including the attempted bombing on Christmas Day in 2009.

AQIM, or Al-Qaeda in the Islamic Maghreb*: Al-North Qaida's African branch, AQIM, principally operates in Algeria, Mali, and Niger.*

The organization has carried out numerous kidnappings and assaults against Western targets in the area.

AQIS, or Al-Qaeda in the Indian Subcontinent: *Al-South Qaida's Asian branch, AQIS, principally operates in Pakistan and Afghanistan. The gang has ties to other terrorist organizations in the area and has participated in multiple attacks on targets in India.*

Al-Qaida has several partners and supporters that support its philosophy and objectives in addition to regional affiliates. These organizations might not have a formal affiliation with al-Qaida, but they might work together on particular missions or pool resources and skills. Al-well-known Qaeda's allies include:

Taliban*: The Taliban is an Islamist militant organization that has close ties to al-Qaida and governs a sizable portion of Afghanistan. Before the US-led invasion of Afghanistan in 2001, Osama bin Laden, the head of Al-Qaeda, had sought refuge there under the Taliban's protection.*

__Haqqani Network:__ The Haqqani Network is a militant organization with strong ties to both the Taliban and al-Qaeda. It is centered in Pakistan. The gang has participated in several notorious strikes in Afghanistan on US and Afghan targets.

Al-Shabaab is a Somali terrorist organization that has sworn allegiance to al-Qaida and has been responsible for several attacks throughout East Africa. The group has carried out several attacks in Kenya and Uganda that were directed at Western interests there.

In conclusion, al-regional Qaida's affiliates and partners are crucial to the *organization's worldwide* activities and a serious threat to both regional and global security.

These organizations are dedicated to carrying out operations against Western targets and building Islamist states in their particular regions. They share the philosophy and goals of al-Qaeda.

Al-Qaida network funding and support

Wealthy people/individual nonprofit organizations, and Islamic extremist groups have all been known to provide financing to Al Qaeda. Besides financial backing, militant organizations and governments that were sympathetic to the group have also provided training, weapons, and safe havens. Several nations and international organizations have put measures in place to freeze assets, track financial transactions, and block financing conduits to combat the finance and support network of Al Qaeda. *Although the organization* continues to pose a threat in many regions of the world, these efforts have been successful in lowering its capacity to finance its operations.

Chapter 4

Al Qaeda's Methods and Techniques

Nonetheless, suicide bombing is a method adopted by terrorist organizations to create maximum damage and casualties by detonating explosives carried by a bomber. The group has been known to use a range of tactics and strategies to achieve its goals. Many extremist organizations around the world, including **Al-Qaeda, ISIS**, and **Hamas,** have used this strategy.

Using violence and fear, terrorist tactics like *suicide bombing* are frequently utilized to advance **political or ideological objectives. These strategies harm society greatly and target defenseless citizens.** Most governments view such conduct as illegal and a violation of human rights and international law.

Attacks by suicide bombers: Al Qaeda has used this strategy to strike both military and civilian targets. These attacks have resulted in severe property damage and fatalities.

Al Qaeda has also engaged in guerilla warfare, employing strategies like hit-and-run operations, ambushes, and sabotage. *These strategies are intended to obstruct the work of the armed forces and government agencies.*

Al Qaeda recruits new members and spreads its ideas **through propaganda**. *The organization has created a significant amount of written content, audio recordings, and films that are shared through a variety of media outlets.*

Al Qaeda has a history of using covert actions, **such as espionage, and sabotage**, to further its objectives. Small teams of agents who work covertly frequently carry out these missions.

Training facilities: Al Qaeda has constructed training facilities in several nations, where recruits are instructed in bomb-making, military strategy, and other subjects. These training facilities are utilized to get fresh recruits ready for terrorist activities.

Al Qaeda has financed its operations through several means, including **smuggling, criminal enterprises, and gifts from powerful people.** Governments and citizens must take a position against terrorism and cooperate to stop the spread of extremist beliefs. *This can be accomplished by stepping up security measures, acquiring intelligence, and launching initiatives to raise awareness and educate the public.* To stop the development of extremist ideology, *it is essential to address the core causes* *of terrorism, such as poverty, political instability, and discrimination.*

It is important to keep in mind that Al Qaeda's tactics and methods have changed throughout time, therefore the organization's present operations could not be exactly what was mentioned above. Furthermore, it's critical to understand that terrorism is a complicated phenomenon with numerous underlying causes and that no one approach or strategy can entirely account for the deeds of any terrorist organization.

Al Qaeda's strategy has changed over time

As it confronted new obstacles and adjusted to shifting conditions, the group changed throughout time in terms of its tactics and strategies.

The following are some significant changes in Al Qaeda's strategy over time.

Creation and early years (1988-1998): Al Qaeda was created in 1988 and its first focus was on aiding and coordinating resistance movements in countries such as Afghanistan and Sudan. The group's methods during this time were primarily centered on guerilla warfare and aiding local insurgents.

The simultaneous attacks on the American embassies in Kenya and Tanzania in 1998 marked the beginning of Al Qaeda as a global terrorist threat. This threat persisted until 2001. The group's strategies changed during this time to encompass more substantial and well-planned assaults against recognizable targets, including the USS Cole in 2000.

Attacks of September 11, 2001: *Al Qaeda established its capability to conduct extensive, coordinated strikes on Western targets with the 9/11 attacks, which marked a significant shift in the organization's strategy. As a result, the group's global image significantly rose, and a large counterterrorism campaign was launched under American leadership.*

(2002–2010) *Concentrate on decentralized attacks: Al Qaeda's leadership was mostly destroyed in the years after 9/11, which caused the* *organization to turn to decentralized assaults carried out by associated groups and lone players. During this time, attacks on hotels and public transportation as well as suicide bombings and vehicle-borne improvised explosive devices (**VBIEDs**) were common tactics.*

***Rise of ISIS (2010–2014)**: With the rise of the Islamic State of Iraq and Syria (ISIS), which was able to annex land and create a de facto state in the Middle East, Al Qaeda encountered a new threat. Al Qaeda replied by turning* *back to insurgency and guerilla warfare while also initiating operations against ISIS sites.*

Al Qaeda has continued to concentrate on decentralized operations carried out by affiliates and lone actors in recent years (2015–present), as well as guerrilla warfare and insurgency in crisis zones **like Syria and Yemen**. The group has also given propaganda and messaging a greater priority, using social media and other platforms to propagate its message and find new members.

The recruitment and publicity strategy of the group

Al-Qaida is a violent Islamist organization that aspires to create an Islamic state on a global scale. It has a history of utilizing propaganda to disseminate its message and gain supporters. Al Qaida has created a variety of propaganda tools, such as movies, publications, and websites, to advance its ideas and operations. These materials frequently show violent imagery in graphic detail, make references to religion, and present the group as valiant defenders of Islam.

Al Qaida has used a variety of recruitment strategies, such as social media, online outreach, and personal networks. Also, it has a history of using coercion and force to coerce others to join. Al-Qaida has targeted people who are marginalized or disenfranchised and may be looking for a feeling of purpose or connection. It is vital to remember that Al-Qaeda has committed numerous acts of terrorism and bloodshed around the world and that the organization is widely seen as using recruitment and propaganda strategies that are unethical and damaging.

Chapter 5

Al Qaeda's Jihad Against the West

Known for carrying out several high-profile assaults against Western targets, including the 9/11 strikes in the United States, Al Qaeda is a terrorist group that first acquired recognition in the late 1980s. To conduct a global jihad or holy war against the West, the group's leader, Osama bin Laden, thought that the United States and its allies were to blame for the oppression of Muslims around the world. A variety of strategies, such as suicide bombers, hijackings, *cyberattacks, & propaganda campaigns*, have been used by Al Qaeda in its conflict with the West. The group has targeted other Muslim nations that it sees as cooperating with the West, in addition to Western nations and their nationals.

The 1998 bombings of the American embassies in **Kenya and Tanzania**, the **2002** bombing of a nightclub in **Bali, Indonesia**, and the ***2005*** bombings of the **London public** transportation system are a few of the group's other significant attacks on Western targets. Increased security measures have been implemented in several nations as a result of Al Qaeda's campaign against the West, which has also had a profound effect on world politics and international relations. Other extremist groups have been encouraged to launch their assaults on Western targets as a result of the group's activities, which have also given rise to several spinoff organizations.

The events of September 11, 2001, and their effects

The September 11th attacks, generally known as 9/11, were a series of planned terrorist assaults carried out on September 11, 2001, in the early hours of the morning by the Islamic extremist organization al-Qaeda. *Four passenger jets were taken over*, and *two of them crashed into the World Trade Center Twin Towers in New York City on purpose*, bringing about their collapse. *Another hijacked airliner* was flown into the *Pentagon in Virginia*, while a *fourth plane crashed in a field in Pennsylvania after its passengers tried to seize control.*

Around **3,000 people**, including *civilians, soldiers, and first responders,* died as a result of the attacks. With **343 and 72 deaths**, respectively, it was the deadliest terrorist assault in history as well **as the most deadly incident in American history for both firemen and law enforcement personnel.**

The War on Terror, which includes military actions in **Afghanistan and**

Iraq, was started by the *US* in the wake of the attacks.

The U.S. government also put in place several domestic security measures, such as establishing the Department of Homeland Security and passing **THE USA PATRIOT Act**, which increased government monitoring authority and raised questions over civil liberties.

As a result of the attacks, tensions between the *United States* and numerous countries with a majority of *Muslims* have risen significantly on the global stage.

In response to the assaults, *stricter screening procedures, and searches were implemented, including* limitations on the bringing of liquids and gels into aircraft. Today's global politics and security strategy are still influenced by the September 11th events.

Al Qaeda's Strikes' Effects on US foreign policy

Long-term as well as short-term, the 9/11 attacks by Al Qaeda had a significant impact on US foreign policy. Following the attacks, the US declared a "***War on Terror***" and began military operations in Afghanistan to topple the Taliban government that had served as an Al Qaeda haven.

To stop further terrorist attacks, the US also put in place several security measures, **such as the USA PATRIOT Act and the Department of Homeland Security**. *Long-term, the 9/11 attacks sparked a fundamental transformation in US foreign policy, with a concentration on counterterrorism and a rise in the use of military force to combat security concerns. With* **wars in Iraq and Afghanistan** lasting longer than ten years each, the US grew more involved in conflicts throughout the Middle East and Central Asia. To reduce terrorist threats, the US intensified its use of drone strikes and other targeted assassinations. *The US's relations with foreign nations were significantly impacted by the 9/11 attacks as well.* The US forged new ties and alliances with nations that shared its commitment to battling terrorism, but many nations, notably those in the Muslim world, opposed and criticized the US for its actions.

Many believed that the US had an aggressive, unilateral foreign policy that ignored human rights and international law.

Al Qaeda's strikes have had a substantial and widespread impact on US foreign policy overall, influencing how the US views international security and how the world views US leadership and strength.

The ongoing threat of Al Qaeda to the United States and its allies

Al Qaeda remains a significant threat to the United States and its allies, despite the progress made in disrupting and dismantling the organization since the attacks of September 11, 2001. Al Qaeda's leadership has been weakened, and the group has been forced to adapt to changing circumstances and new counterterrorism measures. One of the most significant changes in recent years has been the rise of the *Islamic State (ISIS), which has emerged as a rival to Al Qaeda and has taken control of territory in Iraq and Syria.* However, Al Qaeda continues to operate in several countries, including **Afghanistan, Pakistan, Yemen, and Somalia.** The group has also shown resilience and adaptability and has continued to inspire and support terrorist attacks carried out by individuals and small groups around the world. The United States and its allies remain committed to countering the threat posed by Al Qaeda and other terrorist groups.

This includes military action, intelligence operations, and efforts to disrupt the group's financial and logistical networks.

The U.S. government also works closely with international partners to share information and coordinate counterterrorism efforts.

While progress has been made in combating Al Qaeda, the threat remains significant, and the United States and its allies must remain vigilant in their efforts to prevent terrorist attacks and protect their citizens.

Chapter 6

The emergence of new group leaders

The gang can try to take advantage of brand-new security openings or gaps, particularly in unstable or conflict-ridden regions. *Al Qaeda, however, confronts several difficulties, such as rivalry with other jihadist organizations and ongoing pressure from military and intelligence operations.* The gang has failed to recruit and keep new members, and its capacity to carry out massive assaults has dramatically declined in recent years. just when it appeared to be the biggest Islamist menace in the globe. Previous intelligence reports had cautioned that al-Qaida appeared to be taking advantage of a time of relative leadership stability and that the organization was exploiting the Taliban's takeover of Afghanistan. They also warned that al-Qaeda leadership was speaking more openly than in the past. According to a United Nations report released last month, the worldwide environment is in favor of al-Qaeda.

Nevertheless, the report also cautioned *that al-Qaida* "may ultimately become a greater source of directed threat" than its *adversary, Islamic State*. Although al-Qaida used its newfound freedom in *Afghanistan* to establish its hierarchy and line of succession, only a few former counterterrorism officials and analysts warn that there are serious doubts about how well those plans can be implemented given geographic concerns and the growing influence of the terror group's African affiliates. Al Qaida faces difficulties because of this, a former Western counterterrorism officer told VOA while requesting anonymity to discuss current intelligence assessments. The official specifically mentioned worries **about Saif al-Adel, Zawahiri's** longtime heir apparent, that have been shared by other intelligence services globally. **International counterterrorism** officials are similarly hesitant to declare Iran to be a-new Qaeda operational hub as some of their US counterparts are. They point out that despite persistent rumors to the contrary, the most recent information had Ayman al-Zawahiri in Afghanistan. And they contend that the core al-Qaeda leadership still places a high priority on its ties with the Afghan Taliban. Despite Taliban leadership's promises to sever connections with the terror group, U.S. military officers have also noted the ongoing relationship between al-Qaida and the Taliban. Still, the biggest threat comes from al-Qaeda activities in Iran.

In contrast to Afghanistan, where al-Qaeda operated underground in the mountains, al-Qaida is now protected by the Iranian regime's rigid shell. This axis poses a serious threat to international security as well as the safety of the American homeland.

Furthermore, some former U.S. intelligence officials concur that the risk posed by al-continued Qaida's presence in Iran cannot be overstated. Iran had the option of transferring power to their nations. *According to **Norman Roule**, a former national intelligence manager for Iran,* Iran had the option of expelling that facilitation node but chose not to. "It rightly predicted that the international community would take no action. **Roule** claimed that as a result, an increasing number of al-Qaeda commanders and members now saw Iran as a haven that they will eventually exploit. We run the risk of another Al-Qaeda strike on the United States if we do not eliminate this presence.

The effects of Osama bin Laden's death

Osama bin Laden's demise on May 2, 2011, had a profound effect on the world in a variety of ways. Among the main effects are, symbolic triumph in the war on terrorism Osama bin Laden's demise marked a symbolic victory over terrorism, especially against Al-Qaeda, the terrorist group he established. It inspired law enforcement and military professionals who had been putting in countless hours to find bin Laden and other terrorists by demonstrating that even the most evasive terrorists could be apprehended.

Reduced Al-Qaeda activity Al-ability to conduct operations was significantly impacted by the *killing of bin Laden*. Although continuing to carry out operations in select locations, mainly in the **Middle East and North Africa**, the group's capacity to organize and carry out *massive assaults was greatly reduced.* **Security measures** have been tightened up worldwide since the death of bin Laden, especially in nations that have previously been attacked by Al-Qaeda or other terrorist organizations. There were more thorough security inspections at airports, train stations, and other public locations, and sharing and gathering intelligence received more attention. ***impact on Politics Political repercussions*** followed the demise of bin Laden, particularly in the United States. For the Obama administration, which had made the capture or death of bin Laden a primary objective, it was regarded as a tremendous accomplishment.

Also, *it affected US foreign policy, particularly in South Asia and the Middle East.* consequences for Pakistan, Questions were raised regarding Pakistan's participation in terrorism and its ties with the United States after bin Laden was discovered residing in a compound there. A diplomatic split between the two countries resulted from the U.S. government's decision to carry out the raid without notifying the Pakistani government.

The potential for Al Qaeda to reassemble and carry out its deadly campaign

The efforts of various nations' counterterrorism measures, including military action, intelligence operations, and financial restrictions, have significantly degraded Al Qaeda over the years. Al Qaeda might still gather its strength and carry out its terror campaign, nevertheless.

The organization's decentralized structure, which enables it to function flexibly and responsively, is one of the key causes of this. ***Smaller*** *linked groups like Al Qaeda in the Arabian Peninsula (AQAP) and Al Qaeda in the Islamic Maghreb (AQIM),* which are still active in various regions of the world, have helped Al Qaeda survive and carry out its operations. The existence of many ideological and political grievances that the group has abused to gather support is another aspect that increases the possibility of Al Qaeda regrouping. These complaints include social injustice, political and economic persecution, and perceived Western hostility in the Muslim world. Also, the development of new technology and social media websites have given terrorist organizations like Al Qaeda a new channel for recruiting new members and disseminating their propaganda. It is now simpler for them to reach a wider audience because they can engage virtually with supporters and potential recruits.

Although Al Qaeda has lost strength over time, it still retains the ability to gather and carry out its terror campaign. *To keep the group from recovering its prior power, counterterrorism policies must be enacted and strengthened continuously. This entails actions like enhancing intelligence collecting, disabling banking networks, and putting into practice efficient counterterrorism tactics.*

Iran-al-Qaeda relationship

Being the head of Al-Qaeda while imprisoned in a gold cage is not easy.

Together with several other lower-ranking al-Qaida executives, Abd al-Rahman al-Maghrebi, *the terror organization's general manager* and head of its media operations, is said to be in Iran.

Al-Adel and al-Maghrebi are not the only ones, either.

Former U.S. Secretary of State Mike Pompeo once charged Iran of becoming the all-new Qaeda's operational headquarters due to the growth of al-Qaeda officials in Tehran. *However, other American* *intelligence and diplomatic officials have been more circumspect in their predictions,*

characterizing the alliance between Tehran and al-Qaeda *as one of convenience and frequently transactional.* Nonetheless, some observers consider the link to Iran to be problematic.

That does lead to problems, **according to jihadism expert Aaron Zelin of the Washington Center for Near East Policy**. There are concerns about the validity of Iranian sway.

The aftermath of the death of the new leader Al-Zawahiri.

The leadership of the terrorist organization appears to have quietly transferred to his heir apparent in Iran more than six months after the *United States assassinated al-Qaeda head Ayman al-Zawahiri in an attack in Kabul*, Afghanistan. *According to a UN assessment based on information from member states."* Following the attack on July 31 that claimed al-life, Zawahiri's Al-Qaida itself has been silent regarding the situation of its leadership.

Two explanations are given in the report for the quiet. *Al-sensitivity Qaida's to Afghan Taliban worries about not recognizing [Ayman] al-death Zawahiri's in Kabul and al-Adel's presence in the Islamic Republic of Iran prevents al-leadership Adel's from being declared*, the report claims. His whereabouts create concerns that have an impact on the al-intentions of Qaida to exert leadership of a worldwide movement in the face of obstacles, especially those posed by its opponent.

The study further says. Al-Adel has long been considered a potential replacement for *al-Zawahiri by Western intelligence services*, notably those in the US. *They describe the former Egyptian special forces officer as a strong commander with extensive operational experience across many different locales.* **Al-Adel** was a member of a group that began training soldiers and intelligence personnel in **Afghanistan, Pakistan**, and **Sudan in the early 1990s.** He also assisted in the training of **Somalis who fought against US**

forces in Mogadishu from 1992 to 1994 as well as members of *Egyptian Islamic Jihad, an al-Qaeda offshoot. Al-Adel* was charged by the United States in 1998 for his part in the horrific bombings of the US embassies **in Dar es Salaam, Tanzania, and Nairobi, Kenya**, which left **224 people dead** and countless others injured. *Al-Adel has also served on the **Hittin Committee**, which is in charge of overseeing **al-international Qaida's operations**, for a significant amount of time* and is a senior member of the group's

Majlis al-Shura top leadership council. According to the first information provided by **U.N.** member states, the al-leadership of Adel of al-Qaeda has been largely trouble-free. *Al-propaganda Qaida's activities have reportedly grown more sophisticated and prolific"* in recent months, according to the assessment. Additionally, several member states *claim that al-Adel* has been successful in *establishing or extending authority* over a few al-Qaida branches. **Al-Adel** *is allegedly delivering direct instructions"* to Hurras al-Din, one of *the al-affiliates of al-Qaeda in Syria that is headed by his son-in-law, according to at least one member state intelligence service.* But for a long time, both current and past Western counterterrorism officials have questioned whether any al-Qaeda leader could effectively administer the organization from Iran. After the passing of former al-Qaeda leader Ayman al-Zawahiri, a former Western counterterrorism officer told **VOA** that al-Qaeda was facing a difficult situation.

The individual spoke on the condition of anonymity. Does Iran permit him to depart, the former official enquired.

Being the head of Al-Qaeda while imprisoned in a gold cage is not easy. Notwithstanding considerable religious differences between **Iran's Shia government** and al-**roots Qaeda** as a **Sunni organization**, some U.S. officials say Tehran is likely more than eager to aid the terrorist organization. Al Qaeda now has a new headquarters. Early in 2021, Mike Pompeo, who was at the time the US Secretary of State, declared, "It is the Islamic Republic of Iran. At the time, *Pompeo referred to Iran as all-new Qaida's "operational headquarters.* Tehran has let al-Qaida collect money, communicate openly with al-Qaeda members around the world, and carry out numerous other tasks that were traditionally managed from Afghanistan or Pakistan. Some U.S. officials have long believed that Iran's connection with al-Qaida is and has been transactional, that Tehran will assist the terror organization when it serves the goals of the leadership and cracks down on it at other times. Al-Adel may be determined to revive al-Qaeda as a combatant organization to be feared, according to the most recent official assessments from the United States, though getting there won't be easy. The warning from the top diplomat of the United States comes in the final days of American President Donald Trump's term and shifts the administration's attention back to Iran, which it had previously attacked harshly and frequently after Trump's inauguration. *But it also represents a startling departure from assessments of al-Qaeda made just a few months ago by other top administration officials, according to Al-Adel* "Although the decentralized organizational structure is likely to hinder his ability to make quick changes, is probably interested in enhancing al-battlefield Qaida's capabilities, *The Defense Department inspector general* said in a report in November, citing data from the Defense Intelligence Agency. Al-leadership Qaida and the haven it has found in Iran, according to Pompeo, are the very reasons the core group is growing more dangerous. Tehran has let al-Qaida do numerous activities that were *previously controlled by Afghanistan or Pakistan*, including fund-raising, free communication with al-Qaeda members around the globe, and many more, according to the U.S. secretary of state. *Since 2015, Iran has also allowed al-Qaeda commanders more flexibility to roam around inside of Iran with their approval*, according to Pompeo. *The IRGC and the Iranian*

Ministry of Intelligence and Security have offered safe havens and logistical support, such as passports, ID cards, and travel credentials, which facilitate al-Qaida activities. To support his claims, **Pompeo** provided the first ***official US confirmation of the killing of Abu Muhammad al-Masri***, the ***second-highest ranking member of al-Qaeda***, who was shot dead beside his daughter on the streets of Tehran in August, as first reported by The New York Times. Al-Masri, also known as Abdullah Ahmed Abdullah, was one of five senior al-Qaeda operatives who were freed by the Iranian government in exchange for an Iranian diplomat in 2015. Since then, according to U.S. intelligence authorities, he has been residing in Tehran. Letters found in the raid that killed former al-Qaeda leader Osama bin Laden in May 2011 appear to confirm this conclusion made by several current and former intelligence and diplomatic officials.

Global alarming

The threat of terrorism to international security persists, and future terrorist strikes are a legitimate worry. New terrorist organizations and people could form at any time since terrorist groups all over the world are always evolving and adapting to new situations. A consistent and coordinated effort at local, national, and international levels is required to defeat terrorism. Improved intelligence collecting, more security at borders and in public places, and the use of diplomatic and economic means to dismantle terrorist financing networks are a few examples of the actions that fall under this category. *However, avoiding such attacks requires tackling the underlying factors that contribute to terrorism, such as poverty, political persecution, and religious extremism.* This calls for a thorough strategy that goes beyond security measures and incorporates actions to advance social and economic development, advance democracy and human rights, and combat extremist ideas.

In the end, *the war on terrorism is a protracted endeavor that calls for the continued cooperation and efforts of governments, communities, international organizations, civil society, and individual citizens. Together, we can lower the likelihood of further attacks and advance a more tranquil and secure environment for all.*

In conclusion

Because Al Qaeda still can conduct attacks, it is critical to maintain vigilance in the face of this threat. It is challenging to anticipate and stop Al Qaeda's actions because of its dispersed organization, which includes affiliates and followers all across the world. Al Qaeda has also developed and adjusted to the changing environment. Its emphasis has evolved from massive, showy strikes to smaller-scale, more frequent assaults meant to sow fear and unrest. It is crucial to keep an eye on Al Qaeda's activities and take aggressive steps to obstruct its operations and neutralize the threat that it poses.

This includes acquiring intelligence, enforcing the law, and making an effort to interfere with its logistical and financial networks. It's crucial to address the underlying issues that push people to join terrorist groups like Al Qaeda.

Addressing problems like poverty, political repression, and social

inequality is part of doing this because it can foster an environment where extremist ideology can proliferate.

Al Qaeda still poses a threat, which emphasizes the value of being *watchful and taking preventative action to thwart the group's schemes*. This calls for a multidimensional strategy that combines law enforcement with attempts to combat extremism's underlying causes.
Although Al Qaeda is still a threat, it is expected to encounter further

difficulties in the years to come. Its future trajectory will be determined by its capacity to adapt and change, and its ability to garner and keep support in an increasingly crowded and competitive Islamist scene will determine how relevant it remains.

www.ingramcontent.com/pod-product-compliance
Lightning Source LLC
Chambersburg PA
CBHW070738250726
48662CB00004B/1585